For Val
with love
Jerry

Ancestral Lines

Ancestral
Lines

Jeremy Hooker

Jeremy Hooker

Shearsman Books

First published in the United Kingdom in 2016 by
Shearsman Books
50 Westons Hill Drive
Emersons Green
BRISTOL
BS16 7DF

Shearsman Books Ltd Registered Office
30–31 St. James Place, Mangotsfield, Bristol BS16 9JB
(this address not for correspondence)

www.shearsman.com

ISBN 978-1-84861-508-3

Contents

For my brother Tony
and our families past,
present and to come.

'Poems are like ghosts, climbing
into one's flesh, when it suits them.'
Andrew Jordan

Northover Road

1
The sheer quick is a torrent
I glimpse but cannot see.

Blindly
I hold out my hand
and reach for the door.

2

Plums drop on the lawn.
Mating house sparrows fall
on the sunroom roof with a bump.

From the garden
the distant island appears
a blue hill, and far off
across the fields
Fawley Oil Refinery, a blue flame.

Almost blind, my father
sits among his paintings,
colour flowing from his hands.

3

I know the boys playing
on the grass and gravel track
under the tarmac road,
the red-faced angry young farmer,
cow pats and black and white cows.

I delight in the rough plot
where a new house stands –
a pile of bricks
in long grass, the blackberries
and sandy bank, where a lizard lives.

4

Each detail is distinct,
present in place,
yet also a life dissolving
with lives that gave life –
just here – and passing on,
children and children's children
reaching back, moving on.

5

One moment held still:
she called it
Hamlet and the Gardener:
my father with his spade,
hair springing up,
that smile of his, myself
in the role of poet, a young Olivier.

How typical
that she did not
assign herself a part,
as if she were not in the picture,
the one who sustained us all.

6

Young grass fills the ditch,
a bramble reaches out.
The hedge is touched with green.
White flowers on blackthorn.

Walking on the Common
I listen for a stonechat on the gorse.
Water brims the pond, where
ponies stand at the edge.

The stream is alive
with sunlight and shadow.
Poets fill my head with words.

I sit on the bridge with a notebook
learning to see.

7

It's the sheer livingness
I love, and have no word for –
faces, voices, rivers of colour
that are the very walls.

They are not ghosts
that inhabit me
but living souls.

8

Moment before,
moment after, each
distinct, with a fullness
that will not hold.

Some ghost appears,
as if complete,
a bloodless shade.

Each image shatters.
Colour dissolves the walls.
The sheer quick is a torrent
I glimpse, but cannot hold.

I reach
out my hand.
I touch the door.

My parents on their wedding day.

My father painting.

A Love Match

1

Theirs was a love match,
my father said.
Make no mistake about that.

Annie Wastie, from Woodstock,
in service. Tom Hooker, keeper
of the orchids, at Blenheim.

Old photos are a fog,
in which I glimpse, at the centre
of a group of women
all dressed in white
a little man in a bowler hat,
                      tipsy with joy.

2

As a boy leaning on a donkey
he stands by his uncle. Around them,
the workforce of Warsash House,
bearded men with scythes and spades,
women with brushes and pails.

A museum piece, a picture
of labourers wearing smocks
for a social history, page
from a book of life that has gone
as the house has gone, leaving
only a dove cote,
and a flutter of memories.

It is the boy's eyes that hold me
and the tilt of his head,
in which I see my brother.

3

In my life Annie
was a kindness, that disappeared
at Christmas after the war.

I remember my father crying,
my brother trying to comfort him.
In his mind, Dad walked again
grieving, over her old ground,
from Freeland to Church Hanborough.

I sat on the verge of Greenaway Lane
with another small boy, who asked me
who had killed her. Death
puzzled me too, but I knew one
didn't have to be murdered to die.

4

Thomas Alfred was given
the name of a poet, but dismissed
poetry and all the arts.

All, that is, except one –
the art of gardens –
the lay-out, the flowers, the fruit.

5

After Annie died
the little man with a mass
of white hair lived on, and on.

He sent me out to buy fags,
the cheapest brand, which he broke up
and stuffed in his pipe.

At times, the imp of joy
looked out of his face, grinning.

Once, lurking behind a tree,
he gave me apples to bowl
at the canvas, where my father,
easel on the lawn, stood painting.

Love was a word
he never used, until the end,
when he said,
              I loved orchids.

6

My daughter went in search of them,
Annie and Tom, stepping
on paths among gravestones
at Sarisbury Green, reading
the worn and legible faces.

 And there she found them,
familiar names of strangers.
I imagine her stepping lightly,
pausing, touching the rough marks
with fingertips, and finding
what she was looking for, smiling.

7

A face appears
out of the fog, a gesture:

a boy leaning on a donkey,
an old man offering an apple.

One face becomes another
but remains the same,
                    unreadable.

8

Time is cold,
            stone-cold –
a frozen pool.

Her light step pauses.
Her fingers on the grainy stone
feel out the channels of a name,
releasing some strange life,
her own and not her own.

She pauses, spelling
with her fingertips
            two names.

Lightly on the path she moves away.

Evans

1

Love was not a word he used,
the boy leaning on a donkey.

But, surely, he loved his uncle
who nurtured him, and set him
to work with the soil
in gardens of the wealthy.

Hampshire, too, was always
the country he ached for.

2

His mother was unreachable,
a lady's maid become gentlewoman,
a figure like the Queen,
stayed and all black and lacy,
who seldom moved
except with whalebone creaking.

He was the mistake
she had made, the one mistake.

3

Who then was his father?
A man we looked for in vain,
and he, perhaps, never met,
a figure of hints and guesses.

An Evans from Merthyr,
one of the hundreds
and a man of the railways.

He might have worked
for an ironmaster at Dowlais,
or laid rails on tracks
of Trevithick or Brunel.

Or he was a navvy, one
of a gang heaving up shovelfuls
of clay, or blasting tunnels
through the Welsh hills.

4

He appears later as a soldier,
a bandsman
who enjoyed an affair
with the lady's maid
on an Atlantic voyage.

And then he vanishes
from the boy's life, and leaves
another widow in black.

5

I don't know who he was
but sometimes I thought I heard him
in my father's voice
as he sang the old songs.

It was a voice that we –
groaners all – did not inherit,
and he received, perhaps,
from the man from Wales.

6

If I glimpsed him at all
it was in the shadow
of the great ocean liners
of my boyhood,
the mighty steel cliffs
and giant funnels,
the huge, graceful roundnesses:
old ladies of the sea
docked between voyages,
and ready for the next Atlantic romance.

Sarisbury Green Carnival, 1914. The Mould family is in the cart at centre.

Family group at Canterbury House; the author on the left.

Canterbury House

1

Harry Mould was his name.

I liked the old man's blue, watery eyes
and kind, domed forehead.

He came alive for me years later
when I heard how much he loved women.

2

He was a picture to me,
the old man – which at a remark –
he loved women -
he strode out of, or I stepped through,
knowing us one flesh.

I returned then
to that house, once so full of life,
which sickness and unhappiness
came to fill, and through it
the man in his vigour walked
driven with longing.

3

The door out of the parlour
led to a treasure house
of junk – old furniture,
musty books, damp mattresses,
a jumble of china oddments.

Things once belonging to the poor
which only the poor buy
or which gather dust, more dust.

Harry, who collected them
had started poor, born in a cottage
on the Hampshire – Wiltshire border.
Adders climbed the thatch –
he feared snakes all his life.

He was a labourer's son
who became a labourer as a boy,
and grew into a man of substance:
a butcher, owner of carts and horses.

During the Great War
his shires were requisitioned
by the Army, and sent to France.

He employed men
to build houses that stand
with his initials under the eaves.

4

Her name was Charlotte.

Lottie, from Bishopstone
under the downland ridge.
She died, leaving him a young family.
It was as if the world ended.

He buried her in a grave
without a headstone,
at Sarisbury Green, where,
long after, he too was buried
in an unmarked grave.

Harry and Lottie,
one common earth,
nothing to say who they were.

Is it pride that makes a man seek
finally to be no one?
Is it humility?

It is, perhaps, one last
gathering of all he is,
and all he loves – the life
beyond all images, that no one can know.

5

What I know my mother told me.
How she loved him
and hated her stepmother.
How she longed for the mother
who had died when she was a child.

It was the place of her memory
that entered me.

I picture it from the outside,
with horse-drawn waggons
loaded with strawberries
queuing for the London train.

6

The shed behind the house
had been a stable.
                    I tip-toed in,
keeping close to the door.
Mildewed harness on walls.
Windows hung with cobwebs.

I would like to think I heard
the clop of hooves receding,
gunfire from the distant front.
But there was nothing, only
an absence I would not forget.

7

What is our life
but a river of desire –
                    turbulent,
breaking on shallows,
running deep & dark,
flowing out
with a quick sparkle,
and again, vanishing in shadow.

8

What haunts me is the fact
that everything escapes,

the world of things we touch,
even the beloved's hands.

And what of those
who had no life at all,
James, who lived 10 months,
Charles, who had two weeks.

9

Mother in her last days sat
again at table with the family,
all of them together
before her mother died,
sisters and brother, her father,
Harry, whom she always called Pop.

The house was full of life.

10

To me the place was a door.

It opened on ploughed fields
where the boy turned his ankle
on a ridge, so the man
with a built-up shoe
never walked a straight line.

Behind young Harry Mould
scaring crows, or mixing
a flock of sheep with another
on Stockbridge Down,
I saw the fields falling away,
field upon fields, life upon lives.

Sometimes I know
part of him in my flesh,
and the feel of soil
turning under my shoes.

12

In the photograph
we are all together:
mother and father, brothers,
cousins, uncle and aunt.
The old man too, with that look
of his, kind, watery-eyed.

We are standing
in front of the junkshop
which shows part of his name.

Even now, I can feel
the strain in my flesh
as I pull away
from arms holding me back,
wanting to be free, free.

My mother (foregound) picking strawberries
with my aunt and my paternal grandmother.

Rope Hill School rugby team, 1952. The author is at far left.

A View from Marlpit Oak

1

Aubrey, he said, *that was his name.*

He spoke with wonder
towards the end, as if
seeing himself for the first time –
a stranger, his life complete:
a man standing in the light
of all his years –
himself, and a mystery

2

She was a miserable little baby
expected to die,
so they called her Ivy
hoping she would cling, and she did.

Late in life, after an operation
for cancer, she said:
I knew in my bones I would live.

I thought of the gorse stems
after a fire, black and white
and sinewy, like bones with life
compacted in them,
                    unkillable.

3

We will be forgotten.

They spoke acceptingly,
matter of fact, as we sat
by the fire on a winter day.

Strangeness like a ghost
passed through the room.
I was astonished, and afraid.

Forgotten,
Aubrey and Ivy,
no more than ash or bone,
the home emptied,
the house filled with other lives.

4

Time smelt of apples stored
in the garage, broad beans
broken from furry pods,
spuds caked with soil,
sweet peas, night-scented stock.

Sounds too drew lines
forming an interior map –
sparrows mating fell
with a bump on the sunroom roof,
a rush of escaping air
as a train crossed the heath.
A foghorn off the Needles.

One night we heard ponies
in the garden. Dad went down
to shoo them out, and shut the gate.
In the morning we found
he had shut several in.
The soil he worked lovingly
was churned up, vegetables
and fruit trodden in.

Now and then I glimpsed
a moment like a bubble
floating past,
a sunlit raindrop on a thorn.

It was later that I looked back
seeing all from a distant view.

5

Over the rise
the land falls away.

At my back, the Forest,
ancient woodland, open heath.
In front, Latchmoor – a furzy waste
with barrows, ponies
nuzzling gorse, the cut
of the railway – some nights
the sound of a train
would carry me away.

Farther south,
the hump of West Wight.
Beyond Latchmoor,
a gaunt, grey finger
pointing cloudward –
Sway Tower,
a patrician's concrete dream.

Tom once climbed the tower.
He would have seen clear
over the Forest, as far, maybe,
as Salisbury Cathedral spire.

South, an arc of sea,
and, on the Island,
an echoing image, the memorial
on Tennyson Down.

7

Close by the tower
the stream rustles past:

Avon Water, at first
oozing from quaggy heath,
then a trickle, gathering,
finding its many voices.

A power that once drove mills,
it flows dark under alders,
turns a slow eddy,
breaks on shallows,
sunlit, with clear, gravel runs.

Under Wainsford Bridge
it was deep, dark green,
more shadow than water
and so slow it seemed still.

I sat on the parapet staring,
tense with anticipation,
mesmerised, seeing only
what was before me,
transfixed by what I could not see.

Here also I went in love
for the first time, everything old
quick with sunlight,
echoing the river's ancient song.

8

Forgotten.

The living room fire
warm in our faces.

Outside, the day
ash-grey, stone-cold.

My mind gone out,
a wraith of breath

on the emptiness
wandering

9

As I gave their ashes
to river and sea, so
for want of a memorial
I give this back to them.

It is nothing that we own,
this offering,
no plot of land,
but more than memory –
something in my flesh
and in my bones,
a gift of eye and mind.

At my back the ancient woods,
in front Latchmoor,
the living heath
where ponies nuzzle gorse.

Beyond,
the hump of West Wight
like a giant barrow
completes the view.

Cliff-fall house

1

A man walking his dog
might glimpse them passing.

Moonlight silvers waves,
and forms loom, darker in the dark:
breakwaters wreathed with wrack,
emerging or descending.

On the beach
under sand cliffs and slides of clay,
among shingle and shells,
broken brick walls,
a shell of someone's life

and, just visible, young lovers
walking away.

2

We will meet again in dreams
over a lifetime.
Desire unchanging
will fashion changing scenes:

the lyric of being
a mix of memory
and imagined time.

Our initials, J & J
chalked on brick, cut
in wood, but nothing fixed,
invisible signatures
on field and river and wood.

3

Skin to skin
we lie under hazel and oak
or in summer grasses,
eager and awkward
borne on the power
that comes with the sun.

4

We missed each other once.

I crept downstairs,
climbed through the window.
But on the Common, passing
either side of a clump of gorse,
we missed each other in the dark.

I carry this with me
together with a handkerchief
scented and stained with paint
and the first glimpse
of a young art student
wearing a green duffle coat.

5

You sit on the branch of a tree
where I have lifted you,
in your hands sketchbook and charcoal.
All around us, the great field
with the path through June grass,
below, the river valley, an orchard
and the grey tower upstream.

You are drawing what you see.

I see you, and will try
                    to find the words.

6

Sun on sea glitters, shines
on Purbeck and West Wight,
chalk arches of a broken bridge.

On a quiet day we may imagine them:
sudden falls and long ages.

Rivers that moulded slowly,
seas that stormed the land,
laying down gravels and sand,
burying ancient life-forms,
bringing fossil beds to light,
inscribing stories of fiercer suns.

Violent rending,
slow accretion, fallings away
and through all
the blood streams,
        turbulent, dark
shaping new worlds.

7

On a quiet day,
sea calm, sibilant on pebbles
we step down
from fallen gardens,
yellow and mauve lupins
from a border, gone wild
colonise marl and clay
near the sea's edge. Little faces peep
from martins' nests
in the sand and gravel cliff.

The water takes us in.

How cold it is!
Watch for the undertow.
The Island swims
on the horizon, the long shore
shimmers, curves
from Hurst to Hengistbury Head.

Warmer now, our bodies touch.
The sun beats on our heads,
our salt skin shines, we are
one being playing with the sea.

8

It is a glimpse only that he has,
the man walking with his dog;
dark forms looming, breakwaters
emerging or descending,
a little silver that shows the waves,
and young lovers passing
where the broken walls of a house lie
scattered on shingle and sand.

Fairacre

1

Love is first an element,
an atmosphere, a milky cloud

taste & smell & neediness
and then a face, a word.

2

To begin with,
what appears is darkness,
and a dank earthy smell,
mosquitoes whining in my ear.

The blanket I am handed down in
tickles and smells new.
Far off, the crump of bombs –

words I do not know,
but I will learn.

3

I don't know
what I remember,
or remember because I was told

so I hear the Welsh tenor's voice
as he sings opera by the guns
at night, in Pegrim's field.

4

Called in from digging in the ditch
we watch tanks grinding past
on Greenaway Lane, faces
grinning down at us,
hands throwing gum.

One night tanks parked
in a convoy near Canterbury House
explode, and a brave man
drives his burning tank away
saving others by his act.

It was the spring when Keith Douglas
encamped in the New Forest sent out
soldiers to pick primroses to adorn the tents.

Another brave man, a German
awaiting execution in Germany
writes a letter to the future:

you are learning from childhood
that the world is controlled by forces
against which reason is powerless.

5

Standing on the cinder path
Dave holds me up
and points at the sky.

In crossing beams, a point of light
which, as we watch, disintegrates,
and, like a spent firework, falls
in a shower of stars.

6

Innocently the water flows
picking over remnants
of old forests, old wrecks,
new fragments of ruined lives.

The flow is outward:
Southampton Water
to Solent to Channel
to beaches of Normandy.

My brothers are my heroes.
They swim in the river, dive,
white legs waving in the air.

Among crab shells, weed,
cuttle bone, dogfish egg sacs
the shore is strewn with wreckage
and thick with gobbets of tar.

7

I see a bungalow with a red-tiled roof,
an acre of garden, which my father
did not call fair: *as full of weeds
as there are devils in hell.*

But to me it is fair:
a playground with a laurel hedge
on one side, dense with fleshy leaves
where a blackbird at her nest hides,
and on the other, a strawberry field.

A dozen red hens. A trellis
with one tomato ripening
which I pick, because forbidden.
A sty at the bottom, waiting for a pig.

My father with a garden line
or spade, or hoeing the soil
which is thin and gravelly.

8

I dig with my friend in the ditch,
seeking treasure, and finding stones,
sometimes a fragment of clay pipe,
once a shepherd's crown.

Black-headed gulls cry
as they pass overhead:
voices of the river,
of the sea and its tides,
voices that sound with other voices
in my mind, mixing
with what I remember, what I am told,

fact becoming story,
story becoming myth,
myth becoming part of us,
moulding our lives.

9

Love is first an element,
an atmosphere, a milky cloud.

Out of the cloud a face appears,
and then a word.

Afterword: lyric of being

Ancestral Lines originated with a dream and an email. In my dream I entered a small, old-fashioned parlour in which two old women were sitting near a fire in a black, iron grate. The older woman I barely knew, having met her perhaps only once. The other, who was her daughter, I had seen often when I was a boy. She was my mother's stepmother, a woman of narrow religious faith which she preached to all of us. My mother, a loving woman, who had lost her beloved mother when a girl, could not abide her stepmother. From boyhood I too had disliked her, seeing her through my mother's eyes. Later I had realized that I hadn't really known her, and could not be fair to her memory. In my dream, it was now she, the old woman long dead, who gave me a gift.

Near the women in the parlour was a door to another room. This was the door I opened when I woke up, and the door that led into *Ancestral Lines*. It opened into my grandfather's junkshop, which was the front room of Canterbury House. At times over many years I'd tried to write a poem about that house, about the room of junk, and the empty stable at the back of the house, its plough horses requisitioned by the Army during the First World War. The dud poems were invariably morbid, heavy with junk and the emptiness of the stable. They ignored the place that had been so full of life, where my mother and her sisters and brother had been born and brought up, and her beloved mother had died.

Now, at the time of the dream, I was again wanting to attempt a poem about Canterbury House, when I received an email from the poet, Andy Jordan, which included the words: 'Poems are like ghosts, climbing into one's flesh when it suits them.'

The words startled me. How substantial a ghost could be if it were flesh of one's flesh! Yet a ghost that was part of one was no ghost in any conventional sense. As I interpreted the paradoxical idea it came in my mind to combine the mystery of personal identity with the oneness of life. How could one know others, especially those who had given one life, or know oneself apart from them? How could one know the life one was part of?

I speak now of interpretation, but at the time the idea and the dream together caused the strange feeling that a poem is possible, and released the initial impulse that enabled me to write 'Canterbury House'. I remembered the occasion when my grandfather, 'Pop' Mould, had come alive for me, long after his death. I recalled my mother's words, which are never far from my mind, when she said of her mother and father: 'they're part of us, we're part of them'. In this sense, I felt the life of the dead pressing for expression, and bringing, not the darkness of death, but the mystery peculiar to every individual life. The other poems developed around 'Canterbury House', all together constituting *Ancestral Lines*.

Writing the poems, I felt things coming together, a confluence of ideas and sensations and memories. The act of writing released materials belonging to family history – both what I remembered and what I had been told. What 'memory' means in this context may be explained by a passage from my journal, *Openings*, where I describe sharing reminiscences with my parents:

as if memory were in the very air, in the colours & textures of pavements, houses, trees, fields – memory on memory, mine, theirs, other people's, fetched out of time-sequence, rising up at present thoughts, sensations, conversations, but without breaking the one strong invisible tissue. It isn't that we are inside one another's minds, or that individual experience is any less incommunicable in its uniqueness, but the lives lived are somehow together in the places, creating a medium which is as palpable as it is elusive, with an existence which mere dead bricks – places without associations – don't have.

This is as close as I can get to defining what I mean by 'poetry of place' – a term unfortunately prone to sentimental misunderstandings about rootedness. I risked being trapped by such a misconception when I wrote, many years ago, a book of that title. Later, I explored a concept of 'ground', emphasising the material constituents of place, and the natural and historical forces that interact in their formation. Intent on emphasising the sheer grittiness of the concept I may have underplayed individual and shared imaginative reconstructions – the places that live in people.

We exist by virtue of relationships. Individual experience is incommunicable in its uniqueness – as Conrad's Marlow says, 'We live – as we dream – alone'. Yet life only exists because it is shared, belonging to 'the one strong invisible tissue'. 'Place', in this sense, the place of *Ancestral Lines*, is the medium of sharing. The groundwork of the poems is a factual geography and an experienced history, in specific areas on or near the south coast. Their 'medium' is the more elusive reality of shared lives in places, and places in lives.

Themes emerged as the sequence of poems developed. Many years before I had written a poem, 'Near Warsash', in which I spoke of 'another rhythm//… the deep channels/ of married lives'. My concept of the poet was that of one who struggled to keep open a channel between self and world, and the living and the dead, as opposed to writing a verse beginning and ending with the self. 'Near Warsash' and 'Sarisbury Green' were early attempts to achieve this openness, which foreshadowed the theme of love relationships through generations that became a particular focus of Ancestral Lines. This wasn't initially a conscious intention, in spite of the poem in which I first used the phrase, 'married lives'.

Now, the conscious intention came to the fore with memories of parents and grandparents, and the elusive great-grandfather, Evans, and my own first love relationship, which had quickened my sense of the area in which we lived. In writing I sought not memory only, with its deceptive images of past time, but what I call the 'lyric of being'. By this I mean the quick of experience, whether felt or glimpsed: the living moment which, in an image, may intimate the whole life it is part of. The writing came from a sense of connection, not with family and ancestors seen as picturesque figures, or ghosts, but as persons at once respected in their unique being, and felt as flesh of my flesh.

Drawing on family history, on both my own memory and the memories of others, especially my mother, I aimed to reimagine truthfully. Loyalty operated like an instinct: the desire not to misrepresent other people's lives. When I felt there was a risk of this, I cut things out, for example, omitting the figures in the dream which had opened the door to the poem in the first place. These remained as it were in the hinterland of the poem, in the unwritten life from which the poem sprang.

'Married Lives' became the focus of attention. But in imagining them I became aware of ideas and impulses flowing together, as the river of desire flowed through the lives. I found myself writing about seeing, with reference to my father's paintings with their gift of colour, and to the 'fog' of old photographs. Thinking of the reality and mystery of other lives, I felt keenly what may be glimpsed, but never fully seen. At the same time, the 'ghost' in one's flesh has the intimacy of touch.

A friend had introduced me to Michel Henry's idea that life is what we do not see. Henry formulated the idea, but I'd long felt the truth of it. What we glimpse at any moment – in images and pictures, for example – is part of the life-process, in each person, between people, within the natural web, and in history. We cannot stand outside it to see it. Our view is always partial, as our lives are incomplete. But even after death we continue to influence others both genetically and through whatever we leave – memories, poems, paintings, gardens, 'gifts'. If life escapes naturalism, as Virginia Woolf claimed, the 'lyric of being' attempts to touch the momentary quick. Lyric poems communicate the essence of human experience across the millennia, from the clay tablets through the age of the written word.

As themes emerged in the act of writing, so ideas and images worked together. In writing a poetry of place – envisioning the 'medium' of specific locations and events – I sought to avoid the static or merely picturesque, and move with the flow of the poem. Time itself became fluid in the writing, in the presence of lives lived in relation to each other and to place. I knew that, in terms of my favourite quotation from David Jones, I was 'trying to "make a shape out of the very things of which one is oneself made".'

Writing is of course a process of trial and error, of false starts and smudging and deletions. Thought emerges with the poem, teaching the poet to see. *Ancestral Lines* began with a dream that opened a door for me. The door opened on what was ultimately an inexhaustible source – not the past only, but the life that gave life.

The Hooker brothers: from L to R: Tony, David and Jeremy

Acknowledgements

My thanks are due to the late Anne Cluysenaar, Andy Jordan and Philip Gross for reading and criticising an earlier version of 'Canterbury House', and to Andy for the epigraph to the sequence as a whole. I am especially indebted to my wife, Mieke, and to Christopher Meredith for their reading and helpful comments on the entire work-in-progress.

The quotation from the "brave man, a German" in 'Fairacre' is from Dietrich Bonhoeffer, 'Thoughts on the Baptism of D. W. R', in *Letters and Papers from Prison*.

Lightning Source UK Ltd.
Milton Keynes UK
UKOW02f1327060916

282254UK00001B/5/P

9 781848 615083